Creepy Creatures

by Jeri S. Cipriano

STECK-VAUGHN
Harcourt Supplemental Publishers

www.steck-vaughn.com

CONTENTS

Spike-Headed Katydid..................4

Jumping Spider 5

Proboscis Monkey 6

Spotted Bat 7

Horned Toad..................................8

Frilled Lizard.................................9

Three-Horned Chameleon 10

Marine Iguana.............................11

Red-Eyed Leaf Frog....................12

Mudskipper..................................13

Star-Nosed Mole.........................14

Puffer Fish 15

Angler Fish 16

They make you shiver and make you shake.
They make you shudder with each look you take.
But turn the page and take a look.
There are some creepy creatures in this book!

SPIKE-HEADED KATYDID

This insect looks like a creature from outer space!
Can you guess how the spike-headed katydid got its name?
Most katydids eat plants.
But this katydid eats other bugs, snails, and even small frogs.

JUMPING SPIDER

The jumping spider does not trap its meal in a web.
This spider hunts for food.
The jumping spider has very good eyesight.
It jumps on its prey and shoots it with poison.

PROBOSCIS MONKEY

A proboscis monkey has a big, long nose.
It makes a loud, honking sound when danger is near.
Sometimes the monkey's nose gets in the way when it eats.
Then the monkey holds its nose out of the way to chew.

SPOTTED BAT

The spotted bat has huge ears.
It needs big ears to hunt for moths late at night.
The dark night makes it hard to see.
So the spotted bat listens for sounds to find its way.

HORNED TOAD

This creepy creature is a horned toad.
It is called a toad, but it is really a lizard.
The hard spines on its body help this creature stay safe.
The horned toad can also squirt blood out of its eyes.

FRILLED LIZARD

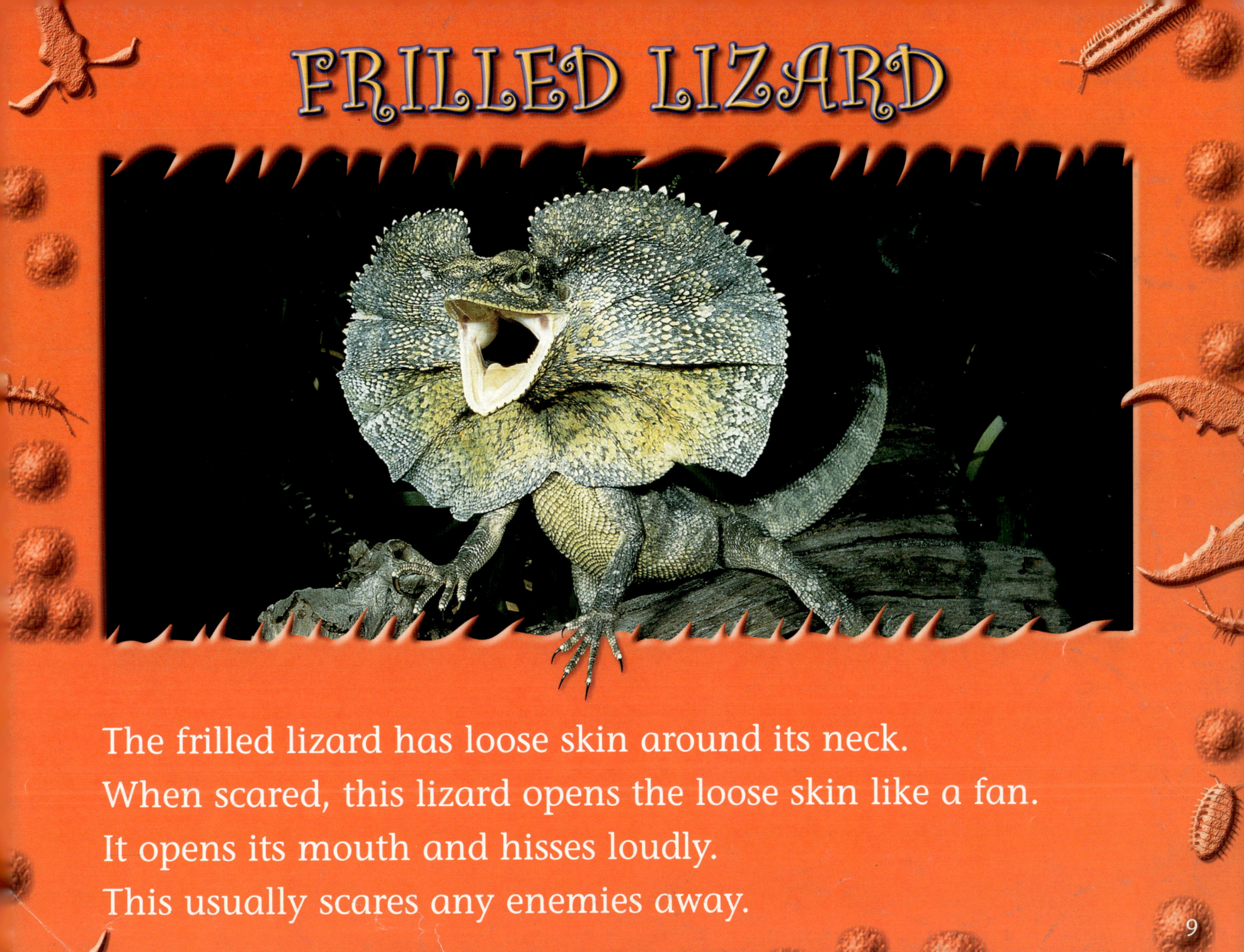

The frilled lizard has loose skin around its neck.
When scared, this lizard opens the loose skin like a fan.
It opens its mouth and hisses loudly.
This usually scares any enemies away.

THREE-HORNED CHAMELEON

This chameleon moves too slowly to catch bugs to eat.
It uses its long, sticky tongue to catch food.
The chameleon's tongue can be twice as long as its body.
Its tongue springs out and back in less than a second!

MARINE IGUANA

The marine iguana looks like a fierce dragon.
But it is really very gentle.
This large lizard is the only lizard that lives in water.
It dives deep underwater to eat seaweed.

RED-EYED LEAF FROG

The red-eyed leaf frog does not like to be seen.
It pulls in its body and closes its eyes when it rests.
When scared, the frog flashes its red eyes and orange feet.
The bright colors scare away any enemies.

MUDSKIPPER

The mudskipper looks like a frog, but it is really a fish.
It moves by skipping on the muddy water where it lives.
The mudskipper can breathe underwater like other fish.
But the mudskipper can breathe air, too.

STAR-NOSED MOLE

The star-nosed mole lives on land, but it likes the water, too.
The parts around the nose of this mole are feelers.
These feelers help the mole find its way in the water.
They also help it know when other animals are near.

PUFFER FISH

This creepy creature is called a puffer fish.
Can you guess why?
This fish can puff up its body so that its spines stick out.
No other fish will attack it then!

ANGLER FISH

The angler fish lives in the deepest part of the ocean.
It has a special rod on its head that glows in the dark.
It uses this glowing rod to catch other fish.
When other fish swim near, the angler gobbles them up.